A BOOK OF HEBREW LETTERS

כ	ת	ה	ש	כ	א
ש	א	י	ר	ש	ה
יי	כ	ש	א	י	ו
ר	ד	כ	כ	ד	נ
ה	י	ו	ה	י	כ
כ	א	ר	נ	ת	י

"Twenty-two letters He engraved, hewed out, weighed, changed,
combined, and formed out of them all existing forms,
and all forms that may in the future be called into existence."

SEPHER YETZIRAH

A BOOK OF

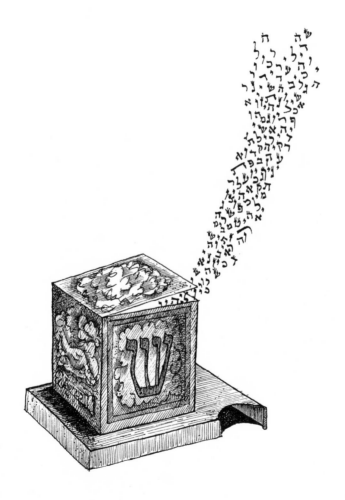

MARK PODWAL
HEBREW LETTERS

The Jewish Publication Society of America

Philadelphia | 1978 · 5739

To the memory of my grandfather
MAX APPELBAUM
who first taught me Yiddish with these letters
and to my nieces and nephew in Israel
ענבר, הלית, מאיה, מיכאל
who use these letters every day

The twenty-two letters of the Hebrew alphabet have long been a source of fascination and wonder to me. As an artist, I have been struck by their visual beauty—a well of inspiration to generations of scribes, calligraphers, and printers whose variations on the letters' arresting forms seem infinite. Most of all, I have been drawn to the rich store of legend and folklore that surrounds the letters of the *aleph-beth*.

The letters, which for millennia have served as an impetus to the Jewish creative process, are in Jewish legend intimately associated with the very act of Creation itself. The Midrash relates that when God was about to create the world, He sought out the aid of assistants. The Torah came forward to offer the help of "twenty-two laborers," the twenty-two letters of the Hebrew alphabet that in their various combinations comprise the text of the Holy Writ. Each letter then stepped forth to plead its particular preeminence. The only letter that refrained was the modest *aleph*. Its humility was later rewarded, when it was accorded the honor of beginning the Ten Commandments.

Further legends speak of the indestructibility of the letters. When Moses shattered the tablets of the Law at Sinai, the letters did not break but flew upward to heaven. Many centuries later, when Rabbi Hananiah was martyred by the Romans, he was wrapped in the scroll of the Law and set aflame. A disciple asked the dying rabbi what he saw. "The parchment is burning," he replied, "but the letters are soaring on high."

Jewish tradition attaches symbolic meaning to each letter of the *aleph-beth*, especially the four letters that make up the ineffable name of God. The addition of one of these letters to a person's own name connotes divine protection and guidance—as in the case of the Patriarch Abraham, whose name was thus changed from Abram by the addition of the letter *he*. Even the manner in which the letters are set down has significance. For instance, great importance is attributed to those prayers and psalms that follow an alphabetical arrangement.

The Hebrew letters are characters, so to speak, in many affecting tales. One such story concerns Rabbi Isaac Luria of Safed and a certain illiterate

Jew. It is told that Rabbi Isaac was once informed by an angel about a man in a nearby town who had prayed on Yom Kippur with even greater conviction and efficacy than the illustrious rabbi himself. Rabbi Isaac journeyed to seek out the man and asked him if he was a scholar. "No," the man replied. The rabbi inquired, "Can you pray?" "No," the man answered. Rabbi Isaac asked, "What then did you do on Yom Kippur?" The man answered: "Rabbi, I know only the letters *aleph* through *yod* of our alphabet. When I arrived at the synagogue and saw how loudly everyone was praying, while I did not know how to pray at all, my heart broke within me. So I began to recite *aleph, beth, gimel, daleth, he, vav, zayin, heth, teth, yod.* Then I said, 'Lord of the Universe, take these letters and make them into words and combine the words together, and may they rise before you as a sweet scent.' That is what I said over and over again." This entreaty, the story concludes, had greater effect in heaven than even the prayers of Rabbi Isaac Luria, for God seeks only the pure heart.

The letters of the Hebrew alphabet are also closely associated with Jewish mysticism. They form the basis for a variety of kabbalistic speculation; special combinations of letters have been considered to wield magical powers, including the calling into existence of "new creatures," like the *golem* of legendary fame. Moreover, kabbalistic teaching holds that by immersing oneself in the twenty-two letters and their combinations, it is possible to empty the mind of all irrelevant subjects that might prevent concentration on divine matters. Thus, the thirteenth-century mystic Abraham Abulafia wrote: "The ordinary life fills up our consciousness with things finite and keeps it in its limits. The problem is, how to open the gates into the infinite? The way to that would be to concentrate our mind upon things other than concrete and sensual . . . on things abstract and spiritual." As the letters of the alphabet are pure forms that have no meaning in themselves, one could free the soul of its natural restraints by meditating on the letters and their combinations. To Abulafia, the letters were stepping stones for ascent to God.

The letters have other exalted functions, among these, to search out novel and hidden meanings of biblical texts. This is done through the method known as *gematria* (calculation), which derives from the fact that each letter also has its numerical equivalent (*aleph* equals one, *beth* two, *gimel* three, and so forth). Through *gematria* words are explained by other words with no obvious relationship other than having the same numerical value. Another method of interpretation is *temurah* (exchange), whereby letters are transposed or substituted and the original word replaced with an artificial equivalent. A form of *temurah* is *atbash*, which involves substituting letters for each other at opposite ends of the alphabet. Thus *aleph*, the first letter, is substituted for *tav*, the last letter, and vice versa; *beth*, the second letter, is substituted for *shin*, the penultimate letter, and so on. This method produces new words, which were often used to "enhance" the magical effects of amulets.

Finally, it should be noted that the letters of the Hebrew alphabet originated as pictographs. This fact, too, is not irrelevant to the series of drawings in this book and to the impulse that brought them forth. Each drawing—or pictograph, if you will—illustrates, in Hebrew alphabetic sequence, a term deriving from Jewish tradition. Above all, each seeks to express, in one form or another, the force and vitality of the twenty-two Hebrew letters in the enduring Jewish experience.

mark podwal

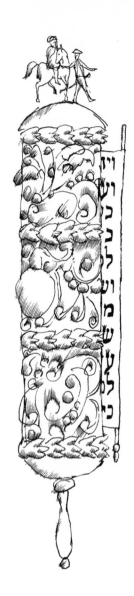

A BOOK OF HEBREW LETTERS

aleph

אלף־בית | ALEPH-BETH
Alphabet

beth

בית המקדש | BETH HA-MIKDASH
Temple

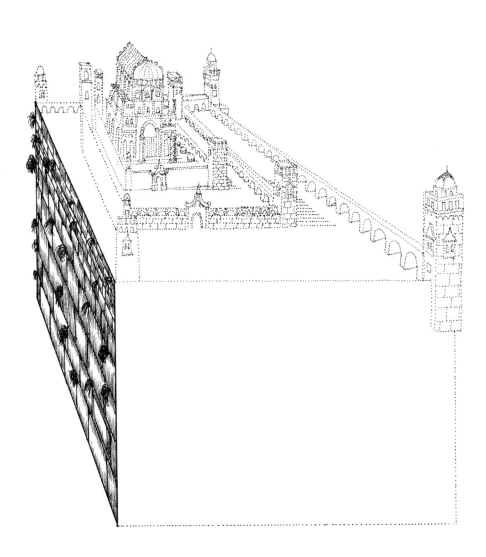

daleth

דרשה | DERASHAH
Sermon

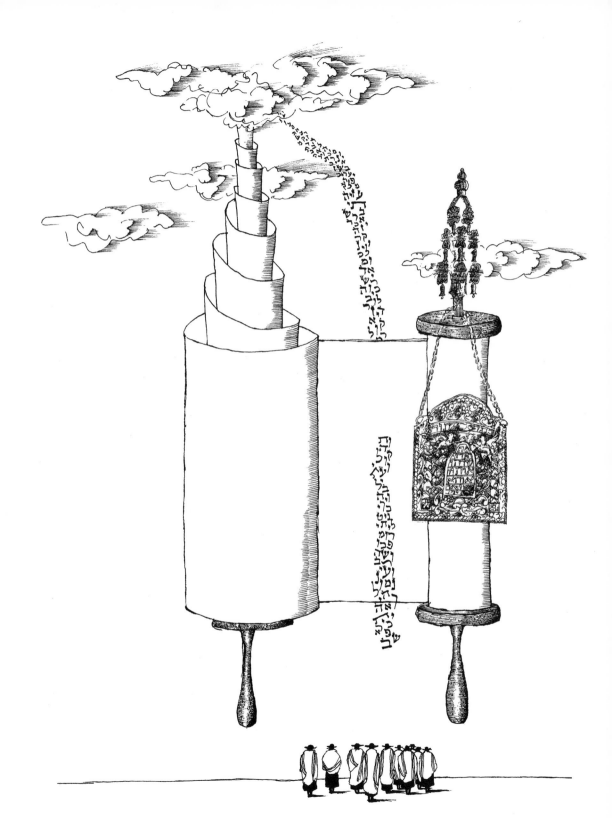

 *he*

הבדלה | HAVDALAH
Differentiation

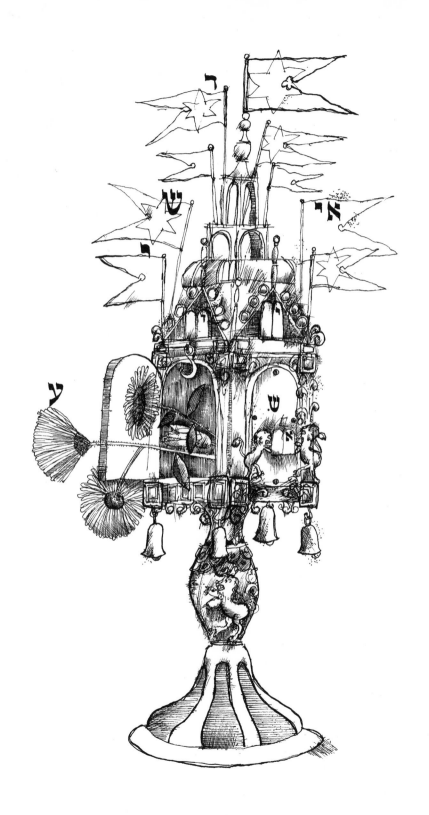

vav

ויהי | VAYEHI
"*And there was . . .*"

zayin

זמירות | ZEMIROTH
| *Songs*

 beth

חדר | HEDER
Elementary Jewish School

teth

טלית | TALLITH
Prayer Shawl

yod

יום טוב | YOM TOV
Holiday

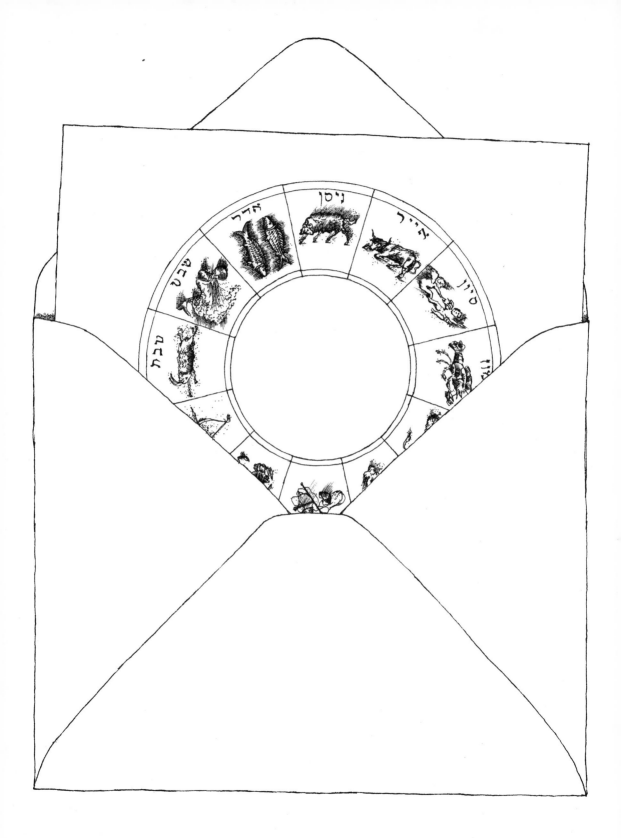

kaph

כתובה | KETUBAH
Marriage Contract

בששי בשבת באחד לחדש אדר שני שנת חמשת
אלפים ארב"ג מאות שלשים ושבע לבראת העולם למנ
שאנו מנן פה בוסיטו מתא דיתבא על נהרי אוטינא וקנאל
מי באות כא הבחור היקר כמר יעקב בכמר אליעזר
הממ..., כמר יצחק עדירא לו הוי ל לאנתו כרת משה
וישראל ואנא אפלח ואוקיר ואזון ואפרנס יתיכ כרהל כפרנ
גברין יהודאין דפלחין ומוקרין וזנין ומפרנסין לנשיהון בקשוטא
ויהיבנא ליכי מהר בתוליכי מאתן זוזי דחזו ליכי מדאוריתא וכסותיכי
וסיפוקיכי ומיעל לותיכי כאורח כל ארעא ויצבאת הכרתה דה
הצענא מרה דא כתולתא דא וחמאת ליה לאנתו ודא
נדניא דהנעלת ליה מבי נשא חמש מאות דוקאטי מעות
חושבים מששה טרין ארביעה פרקיטי איתר מבכנ...ירום
ושלש מאות דוקאטי לערך הגי בכל כד מבליה היינ מזנים
בעצם השישינ לכרה הגי וצבי כבוד החתן צו הגי והוסיף לה
מדיליה מאה וששים וששה דוקאני ושנ שליש דיוקאטי לערך
הגי סך הכל תשע מאות וששים וששה דיוקאטי ושנ שליש
דוקאטי לערך הגי בר סמאן זוי דחזו לה ואמ כמד לא כמד
עקב חתן דנ הגי אחריות שטר כתובתא דא קבלית עלי ועל
ירתאי אחאמריי מן שפר ארג נכסין וקנין וקנקי וראי וזראעד
אנא מקנא נכסי ראית להן אחריות ואגב דלית להן אחריות
כולהו יהון אחראין וערבאן לאחתפרעא מהון שטר כתובתא
דא ואפני מן גלמא מ דל כתפאי בחיי וכמותא מן יומא דנן
ולעלים וקבל עלי כבוד החתן יצו הגי אחריות כתובתא דר"א
סופר כל שטרי כתובות הנהוגת בישראל עשוית כב...ל
תקונו חזל דלא כאסמכתא ולא כטופסי דשטרי. וקנאנא מן
הבחור היקר כמר יעקב חתן דנן בכמך אליעזר סגל צו
הגי לאכת הבחורה הבשטכלי מרה בתולתא דר"א
חמא כת הלוח כמר יצחק נודרא לל מי על מי מאי דכתיב
ומפרש לעי בא... כדשל למקנאה ביה הכל...י וקים

lamed

לחם | LEHEM
Bread

 *mem*

מגילה | MEGILLAH
Scroll

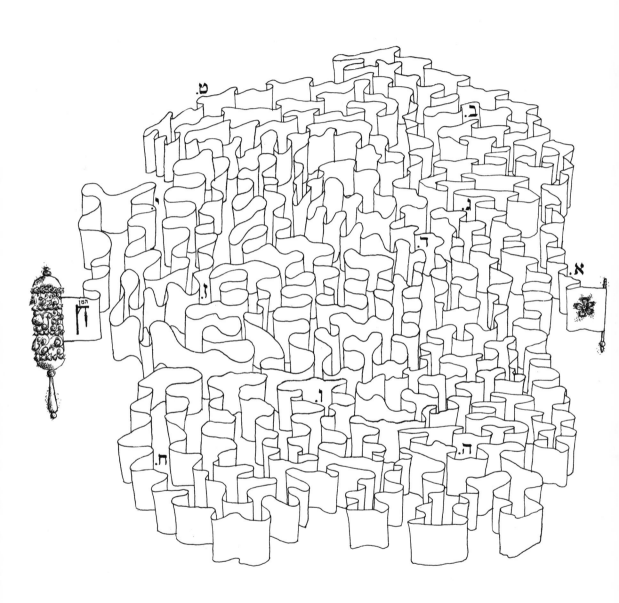

 *nun*

נביא | NAVI
Prophet

 samekh

ספר | SEPHER
Book

 *ayin*

עקדה | AKEDAH
Sacrifice of Isaac

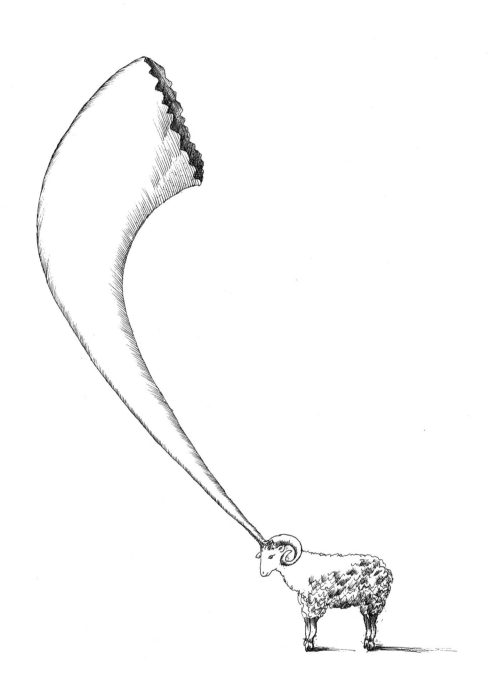

 *pe*

פלפול | PILPUL
Dialectical Exegesis

מאימתי

מאימתי קורין את שמע בערבית. משעה שהכהנים נכנסים

מאימתי הרו וכו׳. פי׳ וכי תנו סבי קריך מנער יום

 tzade

צדיק | TZADDIK
Righteous Man

לו

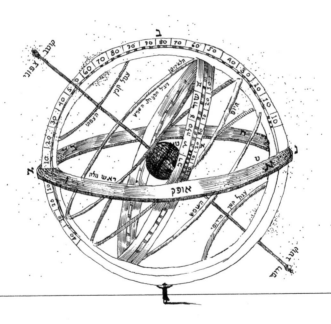

 *koph*

קבלה │ KABBALAH
Tradition

צפת

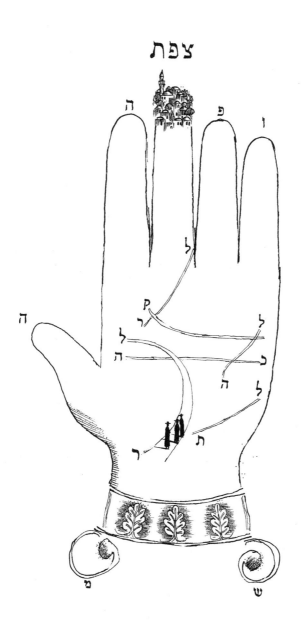

 *resh*

ראש חודש | ROSH HODESH
Beginning of the Month

 *shin*

שלום | SHALOM
Peace

 *tav*

תורה | TORAH
Teaching

NOTES ON THE DRAWINGS

אָ *aleph*

ALEPH-BETH *(Alphabet)*   Every single letter of the Torah is considered so important that he who corrects even one letter in a Torah scroll is regarded by tradition as though he had written that Torah himself. Thus, there developed the custom whereby each Jew symbolically fulfills the *mitzvah* (commandment) of writing a scroll. The *sopher* (scribe) writes only the outlines of the letters at the beginning and end. These letters are then completed in a ceremony known as *siyyum ha-Torah* (the completion of the Torah). The honor is bestowed on those present to ink in the outlined letters.

Although one may touch the parchment of the Torah while writing the letters, ordinarily it is forbidden to touch a Torah scroll with the fingers. Instead, a ceremonial object known as a *yad* (hand) is used to point to the words while reading from the Torah. The *yad* is usually made of silver in the form of a hand with a pointed index finger.

 beth

BETH HA-MIKDASH *(Temple)*   As the only surviving remnant of the Second Temple, the Western Wall was the focus of Jewish pilgrimages through the ages and the repository of Jewish hopes and prayers for religious and national restoration. In this drawing, the appearance of the Temple itself derives from an engraving printed in a Haggadah in seventeenth-century Amsterdam.

ךְ *gimel*

GOLEM *(Robot)*   In Jewish folklore a *golem* is a clay robot who can be magically brought to life in order, among other things, to protect a Jewish community from its enemies. Perhaps the most famous *golem* is the one attributed to the great Rabbi Judah Loew (the Maharal), the spiritual leader of Prague Jewry during the sixteenth century. At this time the Jews of Prague constituted a virtual municipality within the larger city and had their own Town Hall. The tower of this building, which can be seen even today, displays two clocks—one with Roman numerals, the other with Hebrew letters. The hands of the latter move from right to left, "counterclockwise" in ordinary terms but in a perfectly proper direction for Hebrew.

 daleth

DERASHAH *(Sermon)*   For the Torah to be made accessible to each generation, its teachings had to be conveyed to the community at large. A prime medium for this was the *derashah*, the homiletical exposition of Scripture, delivered to the congregation by the preacher. The *derashah* unravelled the implications of what was only hinted at in the written word, rendered the ancient text relevant to the present, drew forth ethical and inspirational meanings, and gave life to the words of the living God.

 he

HAVDALAH *(Differentiation)*   *Havdalah* is the ceremony performed at the conclusion of the Sabbath and festivals, marking the passage from the sacred to the everyday. Blessings are recited over a cup of wine, a lit braided candle, and spices. Containers for the spices have been fashioned from a wide assortment of forms. Among the more popular, deriving from the Middle Ages, is the box in the shape of a fortified tower.

 vav

VAYEHI *("And there was...")*   By the word of God was the world created. *Yehi* ("let there be")...*vayehi* ("and there was")—these are the words in the first chapter of Genesis, which punctuate the rhythm of Creation. There is a tradition that the seven lights of the *menorah* represent the six days of Creation, with the central light symbolizing the Sabbath, the seventh day of rest.

 zayin

ZEMIROTH *(Songs)*   *Zemiroth* are Sabbath hymns, their melodies transmitted from one generation to the next. Some are settings of old texts, some are without words. Whether with words or wordless, joyful or serene, they are the soul of the Jewish Sabbath and express the Sabbath of the Jewish soul.

ב *beth*

HEDER *(Elementary Jewish School)*   In a memoir, *Fun a velt vos iz nishto mer* (From a World That Is No More), the Yiddish novelist I. J. Singer recalls: "One morning, when I turned three, my father wrapped me in his prayer shawl, took me into his arms, and carried me off to Rebbe Meir, the teacher in the *heder*. The teacher immediately began to teach me the Torah, pointing to the *aleph-beth* and chanting: 'See now, little one, the first letter is an *aleph* . . . the second, which looks like a little hut and three walls, is a *beth*. . . . After that is the *gimel*. The fourth letter, which looks like a little ax to chop wood, is a *daleth*.' When we reached the tenth letter, *yod*, he told me to close my eyes. When I opened them, raisins and almonds were strewn over the *aleph-beth*. 'The angel from Heaven has thrown these down to you for studying the Torah,' Rebbe Meir said. 'Eat.'"

ט *teth*

TALLITH *(Prayer Shawl)*   The *tallith*, worn during prayer, is made of silk or wool, rectangular in shape, usually with black or blue stripes, and with *tzitzith* (fringes) at each of the four corners. The wearing of the *tzitzith* is in accordance with the biblical commandment, "Look at [the fringed garment] and recall all the commandments of the Lord and observe them" (Num. 15:39).

    The drawing is of the Tifereth Israel (Nissim Bak) Synagogue, which served as one of the last positions held by the Jews in their defense of the Jewish Quarter of the Old City of Jerusalem in May 1948. This synagogue, like others in the Jewish Quarter, was destroyed by the Jordanians during their occupation of the Old City between 1948 and 1967.

י *yod*

YOM TOV *(Holiday)*   The Jewish year is replete with holidays that range from the solemn to the merry. Originally calculated through direct observance of the New Moon in Eretz Israel, the holidays eventually were fixed into a mathematically calculated calendar. The signs of the zodiac were appropriated long ago by Jews and already appear as mosaic motifs in ancient synagogues. By no means confined to astrology, the signs have been used for a variety of decorative purposes and as Hebrew printers' marks. They are also a common feature of old Jewish calendars.

kaph

KETUBAH *(Marriage Contract)*   The Jewish marriage contract describes the husband's obligations to provide for his wife both during the marriage and in the event of divorce. The *ketubah* is traditionally written in Aramaic, and its margins are often beautifully illuminated. In this drawing, the *ketubah* has been affixed to a wine bottle, wine being offered to the bride and groom in the course of the wedding ceremony as a symbol of joy.

 lamed

LEHEM *(Bread)*   "Mark that the Lord has given you the Sabbath; therefore He gives you two days' food on the sixth day. . . . The house of Israel named it manna" (Exod. 16:29–31). The two loaves of the Sabbath *hallah* commemorate the double portion of the manna collected by the Israelites in the wilderness on the sixth day of the week.

 mem

MEGILLAH *(Scroll)*   Each of the following five books of the Hebrew Scriptures is called a *megillah*: Ruth, Lamentations, Song of Songs, Ecclesiastes, and Esther. However, the word *megillah* by itself usually refers to the Scroll of Esther. The Yiddish colloquialism *a gantze megillah* applies to any long and convoluted tale.

 nun

NAVI *(Prophet)*   "Never again did there arise in Israel a prophet like Moses whom the Lord singled out, face to face . . ." (Deut. 34:10).

 samekh

SEPHER *(Book)*   Throughout their long wanderings in exile, Jews were always most at home in their sacred books. In Hebrew, the title page of a book is called *sha'ar*—"gate," the portal through which one enters the holy text. The twisted columns in the drawing reproduce those found on the title pages of books printed in sixteenth-century Mantua.

ayin

AKEDAH *(Sacrifice of Isaac)*   One of the reasons traditionally given for the sounding of the *shofar* (ram's horn) on Rosh Hashanah is to serve as a reminder of the ram sacrificed by Abraham in place of his son Isaac.

Louis Ginzberg, in *Legends of the Jews* (Vol. I, pp. 284–85), cites the following midrashic exchange:

Abraham: "Didst Thou not promise me to make my seed as numerous as the sand of the sea-shore?"
God: "Yes."
Abraham: "Through which one of my children?"
God: "Through Isaac."
Abraham: "I might have reproached Thee, and said, O, Lord of the world, yesterday Thou didst tell me, In Isaac shall Thy seed be called, and now Thou sayest, Take thy son, thine only son, even Isaac, and offer him for a burnt offering. But I refrained myself, and I said nothing. Thus mayest Thou, when the children of Isaac commit trespasses and because of them fall upon evil times, be mindful of the offering of their father Isaac, and forgive their sins and deliver them from their suffering."
God: "Thou hast said what thou hadst to say, and I will now say what I have to say. Thy children will sin before me in time to come, and I will sit in judgment upon them on the New Year's Day. If they desire that I should grant them pardon, they shall blow the ram's horn on that day, and I, mindful of the ram that was substituted for Isaac as a sacrifice, will forgive them for their sins."

 pe

PILPUL *(Dialectical Exegesis)*   In the fifteenth century, there developed a new method of talmudic study called *pilpul*. Students were encouraged to discover apparent contradictions between various texts and to attempt to reconcile them. Though sometimes abused by becoming a merely hairsplitting exercise, at its best *pilpul* intensified the search for subtle legal distinctions in the Talmud and fostered an appetite for acute intellectual discussion.

The drawing is based on a printed page from the talmudic tractate Berakhot with its major commentaries.

tzade

TZADDIK *(Righteous Man)*   According to the Talmud, there are thirty-six hidden righteous men in each generation on whose account the world continues to exist. There are numerous tales of how in times of great peril, a *lamedvovnik*—the numerical equivalent of the letters *lamed* and *vav* is thirty-six—saves the community, or even the world, and then reverts to his former anonymity.

In the book called *Bahir*, one of the very oldest kabbalistic texts, we read: "A column rises from earth to heaven, and its name is 'just man, saint,' *tzaddik*, after the *tzaddikim* (righteous men, saints). If there are righteous men on the earth, then the column is strengthened. If not, it weakens. It bears the entire world, for it is written (Prov. 10:25): 'The righteous is an everlasting foundation.' But if that column grows weak, then the world cannot continue. Therefore: If there is only one righteous man in the world, he sustains the world."

 koph

KABBALAH (*Tradition*)   *Kabbalah* is the term applied to the dominant form of Jewish mysticism. It originated in twelfth-century Provence and rapidly passed over into Spain, where it underwent its classical development. After the expulsion of the Jews from Spain in 1492, interest in the *Kabbalah* intensified when many Jews turned to mysticism in an attempt to understand the meaning of the catastrophe that had overtaken them. In the sixteenth century the town of Safed, in Upper Galilee, became the center of a new school of kabbalistic teaching whose influence eventually spread throughout the Jewish world.

 resh

ROSH HODESH (*Beginning of the Month*)   The Hebrew month is based on the time it takes for the moon to circle the earth, which is approximately twenty-nine and a half days. Originally, the New Moon was not determined by astronomical calculations, but by the testimonies of eye witnesses in Eretz Israel who had seen the crescent of the moon in the sky. On the thirtieth day of each month, the High Court in Jerusalem would receive their declaration. Depending on whether the New Moon was seen on the thirtieth or thirty-first day, the previous month would have either twenty-nine or thirty days. To proclaim the beginning of the month to the Jewish communities, bonfires were lit consecutively on a series of high mountains. The exact date of *Rosh Hodesh* was important since the dates of the festivals are dependent upon it. Even today, although possessing a fixed calendar, the Jewish liturgy still contains a ritual for the Sanctification of the New Moon.

shin

SHALOM (*Peace*)   "And they shall beat their swords into plowshares and their spears into pruning hooks; nation shall not take up sword against nation; they shall never again know war" (Isa. 2:4).

The Talmud states, "By three things the world is preserved; by justice, by truth, and by peace." Prayers for peace are an important element of the Jewish liturgy.

According to both biblical and rabbinic teachings, world peace will be established with the coming of the Messiah, who is to be preceded by the Prophet Elijah sounding the *shofar* to proclaim his coming. Although he shall be an exalted descendant of the royal House of David, the Messiah himself is often depicted, as in this drawing, as riding into Jerusalem on a donkey in accordance with the verse in Zechariah (9:9): "Rejoice greatly, Fair Zion; raise a shout, Fair Jerusalem! Lo, your king is coming to you. He is victorious, triumphant, yet humble, riding on an ass, on a donkey foaled by a she-ass." The lion dwelling in peace with the lamb illustrates the famous passage from Isaiah (11:6), which indicates that in the messianic age even the realm of Nature shall have achieved a state of peace.

tav

TORAH (*Teaching*)   The Torah consists of the Five Books of Moses as revealed at Mount Sinai. Though man was barred from the Tree of Life in the Garden of Eden after the expulsion of Adam and Eve, he has access to the Torah, which is "a tree of life to all those who cling to it."

About the Artist

Mark Podwal was born in Brooklyn in 1945. His drawings have been exhibited in many museums including the Louvre, the Musée des Beaux-Arts in Bordeaux, and the Jewish Museum in New York. His political drawings regularly appear in the *New York Times* and have been reproduced in numerous publications in the United States and abroad. Among the books he has illustrated are *Let My People Go: A Haggadah*, *The Book of Lamentations*, and *Freud's da Vinci*. He lives in New York City with his wife Ayalah.

The Hebrew letters in this book are written in the Ashkenazi square script in a style developed by the scribe and artist Joel ben Simeon, who lived in Germany and Italy in the fifteenth century.